Take Heart, Seeker

Non-dual poetry revealing what the mind cannot know and the heart has never forgotten

Walter S. Cecchini

Tellwell Talent
www.tellwell.ca

ISBN
978-0-2288-6649-7 (Paperback)
978-0-2288-6650-3 (eBook)

Table of Contents

Dedication

Lovingly dedicated to my mother, Carole,
whose light has brightened so many lives

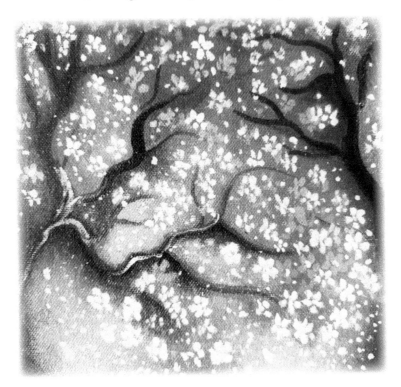

Poem dedications

"*Precious Few*" was inspired by Priyam Saini. Thank-you Priyam for your wonderful illustrations, cover art and steadfast courage.

"*Grace embodied*" was inspired by Grace Roquefort-Villeneuve. Thank-you Grace for your gentle and inclusive presence.

"*Connected*" was inspired by Holger Hubbs. Thank-you Holger for your passion and dedication to growing the non-dual community.

"*A Casual Grin*" was inspired by Charlie Chamberlayne. Thank-you Charlie for the generous sharing of your poems with all.

About The Author

Walter has been interested and involved in spirituality and eastern philosophy since beginning the study of martial arts in his early teens. Operating two martial arts schools for over a decade, Walter felt moved to serve as a police officer and currently specializes in de-escalation, crisis negotiation, and wellness. Walter is teamed with a mental health professional while serving the public, and describes himself as C.O.P. "Consciously on Patrol." Through non-dual understanding, Walter seeks peaceful resolutions and endeavors to provide aid and support to those most vulnerable and marginalized in our society.

Having discovered non-duality in 2018, Walter began writing poetry in March 2021 as a vehicle to clarify non-dual understanding for himself and others.

For information updates regarding "Take Heart, Seeker", please visit *TakeHeartSeeker.com*

Walter currently lives in Ontario, Canada. He is available for speaking engagements and on-line or in-person meetings. He can be reached through email: *Walter@BeingWalter.com*

Visit *BeingWalter.com* to learn about upcoming projects, new poems, and enjoy readings of some of the poems contained herein.

ix

Acknowledgements

A heart-felt thank-you to my family:

Vincent, Samuel, Carole, Walter Sr., Brent, and Julie.

**Thank-you to my non-dual family for
their openness and insights:**

Sylvia Arkilanian, Lowell Arye, Roy Austin, Sylvie Austin,
Kathryn Bennett, Tom Burns, Patrick Bzdak, Derek Carter,
Charlie Chamberlayne, Kevin Harlow, Bernard Champeau,
Sidney DeKoven, Zach Dogar, Ethan Ellappa, Erik Fälth,
Bernadette Fox, Frank Garcia, Jacqueline Gerue, Holger Hubbs,
Mark Jamieson, Leah Kaess, Manfred Knorr, Karen Kreitzer,
Lori Michael, Jaya Miller, Hari Nair, Jason Normandin,
Phyllis Quarles, Nino Rekhviashvili, Jennifer S, Art Sellers,
Grace Roquefort-Villeneuve, Libby Smith, Priyam Saini,
David Spector, George Stergianopoulos, Ana Maria Strandquest,
Kristen Tussey, Lisa Vallon, Monique Verrier, Allen Wagner,
David Wilderman and Guy Wouters.

Gratitude to those who have helped to point the way home:

Adi Shankaracharya, Ramana Maharshi, Anandamayi Ma,
Nisargadatta Maharaj, Sri Ramakrishna, Swami Vivekenanda,
Swami Sarvapriyananda, Ram Dass, Ramesh Balsekar, Papaji,
Mooji, Gangaji, Adyashanti, Michael Singer, Eckhart Tolle,
William Martin, Roger Castillo, Gautam Sachdeva,
Francis Lucille, Jean Klein, J. Krishnamurti, and many more.

I am especially grateful for the gift of having interacted with:

Rupert Spira – *RupertSpira.com*
Magdi Badaway – *MagdiBadawy.com*
The Garden of Friends – *GardenofFriends.com*

xi

Cover Art and Interior Illustrations

Original cover art and interior
illustrations created by Priyam Saini.

Priyam is a visual artist living in Rishikesh, India.

Priyam's works are inspired by her exploration and understanding
of non-duality and express "The One without a second."

Visit Priyam's website at
PriyamSaini.com
to see more of her work and
find a link to her online shop.

Also visit Priyam on Instagram:
instagram.com/priyam_saini

Original custom artwork by Priyam, Rishikesh, India.

Authors Note

Dear reader, this is a book of poetry. *I suggest you skip the introduction, at least for now, and dive into the poems.* The introduction provides a framework for the intellect to understand what non-duality is, the role of the seeker and what one can expect from navigating this path. Poetry, however, slips silently past the sentries and moves undetected by the intellect to find a secret passage into the inner sanctum of the heart. Read and re-read slowly, read silently then read as if you are performing to an audience! Find the unique rhythm of each poem, and allow the deeper meanings to dissolve all that is not essential to who you *truly* are…

Introduction

The end of suffering. This is the claim of self-realization, awakening or enlightenment. The complex or difficult part seems to be shedding the idea that this is in some way reserved for "special" beings or requires years of study. The truth is that it is *simple and direct* for those ready to set their thinking mind aside and 'hear' from a deeper place.

Given that you are reading this it is likely you have questioned your current understanding of existence. Your curiosity is well-placed in that our current view of the world, birth, life, and death - and the very nature of existence - is colored by sensory input and our conditioned mind. A deeper investigation is required into the nature of reality to determine what is *really* going on here.

This is not a 'how-to' step-by-step book but is rather a roadmap urging seekers toward the lowest common denominator: Truth. There is no dogma or belief system necessary. If Truth is true, it must be true for everyone under all circumstances.

It is common for a 'guide' to use the phrase "pointing toward" as it indicates Truth is not a concept someone can explain in words or an idea you can grasp with the mind. Therefore, intellect can only take us so far on this path.

If you asked for and received directions to a place, you would still need to travel to that place to experience all that it had to offer. The directions and description of the place are not a substitute for your direct experience of being there.

Remember the last time someone pulled out their vacation photos to show you? Interesting maybe, but the best-case scenario is that those photos compelled you to travel to and discover that place for yourself and, in doing so, it became your direct experience.

The poetry in this book is intended to have the same effect as those photos, to compel you onward to not only visit that place we poetically call home, but to recognize that you never have and could never leave your true home.

Imagine you round the corner on a trail and come to the mountain summit, the view revealed suddenly, taking your breath away. The beauty observed has a transcendent quality that stops thought and bypasses logic and reason. The result of this temporary stopping of the mind is a peace we may attribute to the event but, examined more closely, we find a setting aside of thought, not the event itself, reveals of our ever-present true nature as *causeless happiness*.

Poetry is especially suited to assist in bypassing the mind as it, on the surface, may entertain and provoke thought but, more importantly, it can stop thought, confound, and arrest the mind, revealing doors and pathways that cannot be found through intellectual analysis.

This collection of poetry is a book of clues, hints, and directions to assist you in finding your way home to your natural state – peace and contentment regardless of apparent outer circumstances.

I would encourage doubt over belief for this investigation. Belief holds us to a concept or position and limits the possibilities that we might consider. Doubt, on the other hand, is questioning something and having the openness to hear more, to keep wondering. Experience is paramount to the investigation we are undertaking here; belief and doubt are both resolved regarding the true nature of fire when one burns themselves for the first time.

The poems in this book speak to seeking, recognition, abiding and celebration. Each could be considered a "stage" on the journey home to yourself. You will find many paradoxes on this journey, and I will suggest to you now that there is no journey to take! While a journey seems necessary, the destination will always be exactly where you started: *here and now*.

I invite you to drop any labels as to how "you" react to the reading of this poetry. Allow whatever arises to arise and come to fruition. Observe the compulsion of your mind wanting to explain or become involved in analysis of "what is going on". This could mean allowing laughter, tears, joy, sadness, and every emotion on the spectrum of human experience without questioning why or from where it is arising.

Embrace the reality that words strung together in a particular sequence are more than the sum of their individual meanings. Reading and re-reading a particular poem and holding its vague outline will allow a deeper meaning to penetrate beyond the cloud of mind into that placeless place, your true nature revealed in its boundless, pristine perfection.

Non-duality is simply the direct and experiential recognition of our One shared being. There are not two beings here. We come to realize that life is not something we 'have' but rather a process, seamlessly and inexorably unfolding and that separation from anyone or anything is an illusion. Investigation of the body and the story that is referenced about "who we think we are" will show that what we *truly* are did not start with the birth of the body and will not end when the body dies. Again, don't believe anything that is written here. Doubt or "not knowing" is the very best starting place when conducting this investigation.

What exactly is a "Spiritual Seeker?"

Everyone is a seeker. Everyone is seeking happiness in whatever way they define that word. A spiritual seeker is simply one who no longer attempts to derive their happiness from the acquisition of objects. An object is anything that can be observed or described. Objects include physical objects, relationships, sensations, emotions, thoughts, and states of mind. Spiritual seekers have begun to distinguish between the real and the unreal, between causeless happiness and temporary pleasures.

There are many pointers and teachings that help to reverse the stretching of attention outward toward objects and trace our way back to our "true nature." This is such a radical shift in the way we have thought in the past that most will not embark on this path. The world will continue to offer its temporary comforts and distractions and keep most moving from one distraction to another and seeking yet another experience.

Poetry points to the path a seeker may follow and illumines the pitfalls, confusions, and the utter simplicity of what is being hinted at.

Plainly put, the mind cannot see what you are. You can never see 'It', you can only be 'It.'

The seeker, the person you believe you are, is one of the objects that must fall away for this insight into your true nature to occur. This is what is meant by the statement "you must get out of your own way."

What is "recognition?"

Recognition of who and what we *truly* are is not an event but rather a remembering of our essential or true nature. The word recognition provides a clue in that it implies a "re-cognition", that our true nature was, at one time, clearly known to us. This remembering could also be called a "dis-covering". We uncover and clearly see that our true nature is what remains when all that is not essential to us is removed.

An example may help illustrate the fact that what we are is ever-present and prior to the birth and death of the body. Creating an ice sculpture of a chair does not change the nature of the water that was used to create it. The chair is 'an appearance' modulated into a temporary form, name and function we assign to it. Once the ice melts, the chair, which had borrowed its existence from frozen water in the form of a chair, ceases to exist. What is left, the water, could be compared to our essential nature. It was present before, during and after the appearance of the chair. We could take the same water and sculpt anything we wish. What we are in our essence, with all removed that we can perceive, is unknowable but is our constant and unwavering self-knowledge felt as Being or the feeling "I am" or "I exist."

Recognition is called many different things including awakening, enlightenment, nirvana etc. Recognition is a common word and therefore a good choice to describe our homecoming. There may be some relaxation in the body or some 'fireworks' in the mind resulting in pleasant or extraordinary experiences however these are 'by-products' of this recognition and are not essential to us. They are merely experiences that come and go, however pleasant.

The 'mistaken identity' resulting in the firm belief that what we are is limited to this temporary body and ever-changing mind keeps us ignorant of our true nature. Ignorance, used in this context, means a forgetting or not-knowing. Through recognizing what we are in our essence, ignorance is removed and what remains is what everyone yearns for – peace, happiness, joy, equanimity.

Some of the poems that follow contain pointers that may cause the mind to fall silent and reveal that which is looking through your eyes to read these words. 'That' is you, prior to mind and the same one writing these words.

What is meant by "abiding?"

We understand what we are not and abide in That which remains. This cannot be called an experience yet there are "happy by-products" of abiding in, and as, what we are in our essence.

The beautiful fragrance of a flower points to something that has produced that fragrance. The perfume of "The Self" or the bodily sensations and expansiveness that come with this recognition may become quite intense and pleasurable and yet should not

be mistaken with that which produces them. You are what you seek! Abiding in the felt understanding of our true nature firmly establishes us in, and as, causeless peace, equanimity, joy and happiness.

There may be a 'back and forth' for many. The feeling of losing, 'coming out' of that 'placeless place' or 'stateless state' is experienced by most even after recognizing what they are in their essence.

Some of these poems serve as a reminder that *we cannot not be what we are* and that each time one becomes lost it is not a sadness in being lost but a joy in discovering and falling into the love that we are all over again!

The question has been posed "and so now what"? What does one do after establishing oneself as a "knower of reality"?

Simply put, this question does not arise for one who has recognized what they are and is "steady in wisdom."

This steadiness implies that one no longer completely loses themselves in the world and again becomes identified with narrative, regrets of the past or projections of the future. They no longer identify as "the person" and story but rather as the "one being" we share. They understand and experience they are but one "point of view" existence uses to view itself.

Celebration is to have this understanding, this recognition of your true nature, inform *every* interaction you are involved in. Actions and words coming from this 'place' are incapable of lower behaviors regardless of the outcome. Mind is no longer involved in scheming and judging and ceases to compulsively react. Responses to and interactions with *apparent* others are out of love and compassion. The word 'apparent' used here speaks to this recognition revealing that separation is an illusion. As stated earlier, there are 'not two'

beings here and our interactions are now known to be only ever with the One being that we share.

Established in this understanding there is no person who "gets it." There is no separation, no sense of lack or loneliness, only of peace and contentment irrespective of apparent "outside" circumstances.

Walter Cecchini
August 2021

Take Heart, Seeker

You may be filled with longing
but take heart, seeker,
this longing guides you
and the wind is at your back

You may grow weary
but take heart, seeker,
your destination
could not be closer

You may feel lost
but take heart, seeker,
you could never go
where This is not

You may feel doubt
but take heart, seeker,
doubt is for believers,
trust only your experience

Your mind may be confused
but take heart, seeker,
your mind cannot know
what your heart has never forgotten

You will never be free
but take heart, seeker,
freedom is not for the seeker
but for the One who is sought

Take heart, dear seeker,
for you are that One.

By The Fire

If what you came here for
was another morsel of knowledge,
a candy for the mind to chew on,
then take leave and seek elsewhere
for tasty shortcuts that keep you wanting more.

~

If what you came here for
started as a longing
and became a burning fever,
threatening to ignite your insides...
Then come sit here,
by the fire.

A to B

Prepared for my journey I take up my pack,
with map at the ready there's no turning back

I step out the door leaving 'A' bound for 'B'
and promptly get lost, arriving at 'C'

Consulting my map, a stream marks the way,
but I find a wild river swollen from rain

Unable to cross, I set out for 'D',
the map showing now a gnarled old tree

Instead of a tree I find an old man
who laughs at my efforts and the thought of a plan

He offers a clue to help guide my way,
to arrive safely at 'B' by the end of the day

"Forget what you seek and journey unbound,
for what you are seeking can never be found!

What you call 'B' is not a thing to behold,
more common than dirt more precious than gold!

Turn around and go back but not to a place,
arrive nowhere to find the end of your race!"

I set off at a run from this crazy old coot
'B' must be out there, I just need a new route.

Yeah, but...

As one would expect
a question was posed,
the teacher responded
and another arose.

Again, words pointed
to ineffable Truth
but the student protested
demanding more proof.

Gently nudging the student
toward that which is here,
the teacher attempted
to make it more clear.

The student sat puzzled
and exclaimed yet again,
and like a patient grandparent
the teacher weighed in.

When the session had ended,
the case open and shut,
all the student had left
was a feeble "Yeah, but…"

Welcome

I woke up this morning and heard a voice say
there is sadness felt in this body today

Misery loves company and soon it was known
that sadness invited some friends of its own

Grief and sorrow came through the door,
shame curled up in a ball on the floor

Why or from where they arrived is not clear
regardless of that, I welcomed them here

I sat with them quietly, did not interfere
as each said their piece tinged with longing and fear

When lunch came around I offered a bite
but each remained silent perhaps out of spite

Later, out for a walk I noticed a bird,
the most beautiful song was gratefully heard

I realized then that my guests had all gone,
I turned back to the sun which through it all shone

They may all return unbidden, who knows?
but one thing is certain, they'll eventually go

Thing-less

Is happiness baked
into a cookie or cake?
Does the recipe call
for a dash or a shake?

Will happiness be
a part of the deal
when you're handed the keys
to your new set of wheels?

Can happiness come
from one you meet
who sweeps you away
right off of your feet?

If somehow you see
the answer is no...
Then where does it come from?
And where could it go?

A clue to this riddle
begins with desire and
clear seeing that wanting
fuels the fire

An insatiable void
that no thing can fill,
constant seek and avoid
will leave us quite ill

It's within your power
to alter your course,
shine the light of awareness
back in on its source

The mind will attempt
to tag along for the ride
but can never keep up,
remaining outside

Known but not found,
always hidden from view,
is where happiness lives...
in fact, it is you!

Here it is known
an unending spring,
no objects to speak of,
no thing called a thing

Arithmetic

For the seeker it seems
this problem complex,
with cryptic instructions
that leaves them perplexed

So back we will go
to the primary grades
and revisit some ideas
still useful today

Addition was first,
two plus two equals four,
we discard this concept
as it always yields more

Division we know
and we do every day,
our judgements divide,
let's throw this away

Multiplication of problems
occurs when the mind
believes it controls,
best leave this behind

Subtraction is last,
the most useful of math,
remove every last thing,
even the path

What remains in this moment
when this process is done?
Is there anything left,
is there even a one?

In fact there is nothing,
no more homework to do
except subtract subtraction.
Can you find one called you?

Distracted

Walking up a hill
I see the light shining
just over the other side

What beautiful flowers!
I stop and pick a bunch,
not wanting to part from them

I continue walking
drawn magnetically upwards,
the light urging me forward

A cramp in my foot!
I stop a while to give
attention to the pain

Walking on,
I sense the light
warm and inviting

I think I hear a noise!
A rustling in the bushes...
I search but find no one

Walking now I grow tired
and lie down to sleep.
I dream of the light.

The Gadabout

Be wary of the knock at the door
and the arrival of the gadabout
who brings tourist-trap trinkets
and scandalous news of the world

This charlatan creates unease
by filling silence with blather,
misrepresenting you to others
and speaking out of turn

Entertaining this one,
listening to their stories,
will invite them to stay longer
and to call your house their home

Keeping ready the finest room
for this world-weary vagabond
relegates you to quarters
unbecoming of the landlord

Leave the front door unlocked,
allow the comings and goings,
but withdraw your hearty welcome
and dispense with fanfare

Attend to the one
who never arrived,
who will never leave.
The one you call "I"

'NoW Here'

Preparing a meal
with the exacting precision
of a surgeon
operating to save a life.

Eating the meal
with the rapt attention
of a skydiver
packing their parachute.

Washing the dishes
with the delicate care
of an archeologist
unearthing ancient fragments.

Preparing tea
with the unwavering focus
of an artist
finishing a masterpiece.

Walking in the forest
with all the curious wonder
of an astronaut
exploring an unknown planet.

Attention to now
with the complete openness
of Awareness
aware of Awareness.

Welcome to 'NoWHere.'

Maya

I met a girl named Maya,
so beautiful and kind,
that when she showed her darker side
I really didn't mind.

She held me in her thrall,
kept me at her whim,
striving to keep up with her
was more like sink than swim.

Fortune came and fortune went,
great suffering ensued,
when Maya offered more and more
I began to come unglued.

Gazing at her lovely face,
her mouth twisted in a scowl,
I struggled to make sense of this,
so fair and yet so foul!

This story ends for most of us
in a bitter-sweet kind of way...
Maya's charms are all we know,
thus, in ignorance we stay.

The other ending possible
is exceedingly quite rare:
see through Maya's illusion,
to know what's really there.

Neutral-Eyes

May your sight remain
prescription-free
with no lenses added
to change what you see

I speak not of
your physical eyes
for your vision will blur
as quickly time flies

I refer to all senses
that report to that One…
awareness unfiltered,
the illumining sun

Clear seeing adds nothing
to the experience of sight
but remains free of conditioning
and limiting blight

A newborn's experience
begins in this way
no beliefs, expectations
or fear to hold sway

Observe the world
with the eyes of a child
with no need for narrative
and again be beguiled!

Clear seeing reveals beauty
as music and art
and dancing and laughter,
a wide-open heart.

Keep Quiet

This elusive, ineffable, unutterable truth

defies expression through verbal allusions

and confounds the most profound communicators,

erudite orators appear as confabulators!

~

The answer comes easily and in a moment,

comes with the willingness to drop busy-ness,

to overlook the movement of the mind.

I am trying to be kind when I say: keep quiet.

About Nothing

Let's talk about nothing,
sounds funny to say,
however, this discourse
whisks all questions away

Away to where?
To nowhere of course,
in the absence of objects
we abide in the source

How do we get there?
Drop every last thing,
what remains is nothing,
to no-thing we cling

Removing attachments,
nothing to hold,
just be what you are
and observe life unfold

This unlocated location
in nowhere it hides,
infinite potential,
timeless, no size

The more that is said
takes us further away,
let's sit here in silence,
there's nothing to say

Teachers

Walking in the forest
we may take notice of teachers
who impart lessons
to anyone willing to listen.

Trees stand tall,
welcoming the wind,
swaying, flexing, bending,
partners in a timeless dance,
a soundtrack of birdsong
and rushing water
and rustling leaves.
Trees, noble,
do not know
they are noble.

Rocks sit silently,
imperturbable, enduring,
seemingly immutable
yet mutable, yielding
to the gentle caress
of a mountain stream
smoothing and shaping.
Rocks, utterly still,
do not know
they are still.

Animals move about
not imagining or planning
where or how or when,
yet, life provides
and requires no desire.
Things are as they are.
Animals do not wish or hope
for this moment to be different.
Animals, surrendered,
do not know
they surrender.

Embracing these teachings
we stand, sit, move.

Noble, still, surrendered.

Not knowing.

Dream'I'ng

I had a dream that seemed so real,
it's quite a story to tell

In short, I dreamt that I didn't exist,
my body an empty shell!

I sensed a presence that seemed to glow
in the background of all I felt

It never spoke yet it was quite clear
that as it grew, I would melt

I was terrified I would disappear,
an imposter taking my place

But as time went on, I felt more peace
with a radiant smile on my face

The last thing I remember before I awoke
was that I knew I could never die

It was then I remembered who I've always been
and that my real name is simply 'I'

The lingering feeling I'm experiencing now
is the sense that my dream is true

And I'm left with a puzzle not yet figured out,
.....just who does this 'I' refer to?

Tracing Back

Viewing the world, I use eyes to see,
all that appears, separate from me

Yet mind sees these eyes and so they must be
objects perceived - only through which I see

My mind too is known and here is the key,
what knows my mind is what I must be

I trace my way back, and abide in that one,
which reveals my essence, a radiant sun

What is discovered is not confined to a place,
I return to the world and see my true face

For no object exists in its own right,
only borrows its form from my glorious light

Yet most still feel as if they exist
in the world of ideas, the obvious missed

But now I see you, having traced your way back,
no distance between us and nothing we lack.

Safe Harbor

It's time to shelve the books
having recognized that
swimming requires entering the water

Life does not allow you to wade in
but drops you into the turbulent ocean
with roiling waves and no land in sight

Having shed the weight of identity,
you find now that you are naturally buoyant,
swimming in the ocean of existence is effortless

Others around you flounder and cry for help,
refusing to let go of their burden,
clutching objects as they choke and sputter

A desperate, drowning swimmer
wraps their arms around your neck,
their weight threatening to drag you under

The momentary panic you feel is seen
from a safe harbor and you realize
that your feet could touch bottom all along

In this instant of recognition, you transform
from buoy to lighthouse, a beacon guiding others
from darkness and death to light and life

Chase No More

The sharpest mind
cannot impart
any matter
of the heart

~

Facts and figures
do not comprise
understanding
of the wise

~

Ownership
does not last
as every-thing
will surely pass

~

Accolades
will not endow
any greater
sense of now

~

Chase no more,
end your strife,
recognize that
YOU are life!

And Know

We few who are interested will speak of this,
wielding clunky words,
stretching metaphors over that which cannot be covered,
only pointed at with crooked fingers,
hinted at with clever analogies,
dancing with wild abandon
dangerously close to the campfire,
no real facts, only myth and legend,
stating 'thou art this' and 'thou art that.'

Each recognizes what they are
and what the others are.

And so,
words exhausted,
we sit as a whole,
in stillness,
in silence...

And know.

Anahata

The news is not all doom and gloom
as this seeming regression of humanity
can be a catalyst for those seeking Truth

Truth has always been, and is always available,
but overshadowed for most by the societal mind
in the form of news outlets, internet, and social media

Your openness to hearing this message includes you in
a growing audience who is turning down the volume
and allowing the light of Truth to expose this 'fake news'

Turning inward reveals the sweet and pervasive silence
that makes all, even the cacophony, possible,
delving down to the heart of the matter

This revelation is not made by adjusting the dial
but by switching roles from receiver to transmitter
and once again turning outward to the world

Anahata, the unstruck, primordial sound of existence
is amplified effortlessly by the presence of realized beings,
an equanimous healing broadcast for the benefit of all

Dear John

I hope this letter answers
all your questions as to why,
I'm telling you it's time to part
and somehow say goodbye.

I have watched you from your very start,
while you formed your current ways,
seeking pleasure and avoiding pain
has filled your earthly days.

You keep saying that you'll improve
with effort and with time,
but trust me John I know, too well,
the limits of your mind.

Your need to control, to steer your life
has brought suffering and tears,
repressed emotional energies
compound your phantom fears.

You somehow think a vacation or ring
will bring you closer to your goal,
but dearest John, you've missed the point,
you are already whole!

In closing, I know you may be lost,
so I have some advice to share:
it may be easier to find your place
if you see you were never there.

I remain,

Your True Nature

Abundance First

With bills to pay
and mouths to feed
there always seems
to be a need

Comparing ourselves
to the folks next door
will drive our desire
to seek more and more

Buried deep within
the pain of lack
sends us into the world
to bring objects back

Any movement out,
any distance away
increases our longing
as we wander and stray

There exists however
another way
to fill the void
that grows each day

A different angle,
a perspective shift,
and we start to sense
a most valuable gift

Sinking deeper within,
breaking the curse,
we soon come to see
that abundance comes first

In the heart of the self,
pure potential distilled,
nothing to seek,
all desires fulfilled

A clear understanding
ends striving and strife
with all we require
provided by life.

Adversity

Faced with each adversity
Truth will not negate
the challenges that appear to us
but will transform how we relate

Remaining still as life unfolds
in silence beyond mind,
we meet each seeming obstacle
resistance left behind

Suspended within infinity,
this body held by grace,
our expectations and entitlements
lose their lofty place

Experiencing pain in any form
grants a chance to see
that suffering is optional
and with this we are free

Make use of every stumbling block
that the mind may term unfair,
find refuge in eternal Self
that not-as-two we share

Unbecoming

Delusions fall like lumps of clay

as the potter shapes and molds

what once was thought to be separate,

the body known now to not only contain

but be contained within the whole,

a unique viewpoint through which

the potter gazes upon creation.

No person survives this unbecoming.

No Matter

No matter where I look I see
reflections looking back at me

No matter what I reach to touch
I find myself and feel as much

No matter what my ears might hear
in me those sounds all appear

No matter what tastes may delight
all are revealed by my light

No matter what this nose may smell
sweet or pungent, to me it tells

No matter what thoughts rise and fall
I watch them pass, one and all

Who am I that knows these things?
Know thyself, O King of Kings!

Spring Cleaning

My picture of how things ought to be
I have constructed carefully

Yet the outside world is not aligned
with what I hold inside my mind

How dare the world now present
what I don't prefer and do resent!

Resistance arises to what is here,
thoughts, feelings, emotions all appear

This tangled mess of energy
is not something I want to see

With force of will I push it down
beneath, behind, and underground

I add it to the suppressed glob
that grows like an unruly mob

It poisons all life's interactions
divides, separates, creates factions

What I have pushed down so deep
appears as dreams that haunt my sleep

The mind's projections of this mess,
are not a fix, just restless rest

By grace and discernment, I begin to see
that glob of tar… it isn't me

When I turn my gaze toward that "thing"
Awareness begins the melt of spring

Slowly and with courage now,
I release that which I had bound

I let go and experience relief,
let go of anger, sadness, grief

Moving on from this point
I dismantle preferences joint by joint

I erase my expectations of how
Life should unfold - this is my vow

For Nature paints just as She will
and knowing my desires mean nil

I relax, sit back, enjoy the show…
Nothing to do, nowhere to go.

We Are Filled

Silence fills space,
inner and outer.
Yet there are not
two spaces here;
an undivided whole.

As space pervades
everything,
silence spans
vast distances or a
schism between two minds.

As water assumes
the shape of a vessel,
silence allows
the sounds of
peace or mayhem.

As mind imagines
myriad scenarios,
silence holds
past or future
in this eternal moment.

Listen, not with attention, but as attention.
Hear, not with intellect, but as knowing.

Listen.

Remaining empty,
we are filled.

Sweet Repose

Unbiased, objective seeing
reveals unqualified, unborn Being.

~

Known yet without shape or size,
outside space, outside time.

~

Seek until the seeker dies
and rest beyond the cloud of mind.

~

All are welcome yet few will know
the joy and peace of sweet repose.

In, and As, Freedom

When I first saw the butterfly
I was captivated by its beauty,
desire rising to possess it,
a thing to be owned.

I tried to capture it
but could not,
it flowed freely,
meandering unpredictably.

I tried to follow it
but failed,
its movements effortless
while I struggled to keep up.

Exhausted, I sat in a meadow
as the sound of a brook
and sensation of a soft breeze
dissolved my desire.

I opened my eyes to find
the butterfly perched
on the back of my hand,
light and gentle.

Wings moving slowly,
wordlessly expressing
that we belong to only One,
in, and as, freedom.

The Flower

Silence is the medium
in which Being reveals
its ubiquitous presence
as happiness and contentment.

~

Few will withstand distraction,
as the mind is piqued
by the intense fragrance
emanating from source.

~

Rare are those
who step out of the way
when the mind charges
into analysis and ownership.

~

Enjoy the fragrance
but be not satisfied
until you sit
as the flower itself.

Sitting Alone

Sitting alone,
I am not lonely.
There are no others
I could miss.

Sitting alone,
I am fulfilled.
There is no thing
I could desire.

Sitting alone,
I am at home.
There is no other space
I could go.

Sitting alone,
I am.

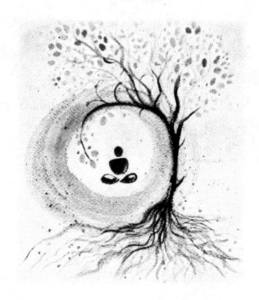

In This Moment

In this moment I am not

answering to a name or recalling an identity,

referring to the past or imagining a future,

looking for or shunning any experience,

seeking to understand or be understood,

ignoring or embracing sensations.

In this moment, all seeking ends.

In this moment, I am.

I Abide

The light shines,
unseen yet seen
as the world beckons,
a grand exhibition
to tempt the senses.

~

I abide, observing
the comings and goings,
the empty promises that
ring hollow.

~

I remain gazing inward
toward the source of all,
a quiet vigilance,
a peaceful surrender,
honoring That which is
and can never not be.

Borderless

We welcome the arrival
of what we call "flower"
then lament its withering,
longing for the decaying lump
to be what it once was,
to meet our expectations,
sweet fragrance and vibrant colors

~

Yet we never hold a thing
called "flower" in our hand,
we cling to a momentary
appearance of life in flux,
temporarily modulated
into a nameless flow
delicate and fleeting.

~

Regarding this "flower"
but dropping the label,
we understand life is a process,
"flower" and "I" borderless,
inseparably dancing,
a seamless happening,
endless expression!

Turn Around

Having dipped your toes
into the infinite ocean,
causing your breath to
hitch and catch
and your mind collapse,
the present moment revealed,
pure and unalloyed…

Having disappeared
for even a second
to that placeless place
and timeless time,
an indelible impression
of perfection beyond form
stamped on the periphery of your mind…

Having remembered your true nature,
could you continue to allow
your senses to run amok
drawing you toward transience,
making investments in impermanence,
being controlled by mind,
and choosing suffering over peace?

Having found your way home,
turn around
and end the quest
to find what was not lost,
to reveal what was never hidden,
to embrace what has always held you
and disappear, into yourself.

Back to Basics

The shedding of all
that is not essential to us
reveals our innate goodness,
prior to rules, laws, and customs.

A smile requires no translation,
a silent indication
of our inward state,
inclusiveness.

A good deed needs no interpretation,
a gentle lifting,
reinforcing our common bond,
acknowledging worth.

Listening to others speak,
offering time and attention,
a passive confirmation,
a validation.

Moving through the world
we remain in our essence
our basic, innate goodness
revealed in every move.

Like Space

I am like space,
I cannot be seen.
Yet, here I am,
ever-present.

I am like space,
I cannot be understood,
named or examined,
without attributes.

I am like space,
in which all appears,
borderless,
infinite.

I am like space,
no beginning or end,
always now,
eternal.

I am like space,
silent and still,
luminous,
aware.

Silence is Heard

Words are put to the test
shadows of truth at best
when one attempts to say
anything in any way

We've heard
'never say never,
never say always,'
as the saying goes

And in saying this
we take a risk
when we think
it is truth we know

So do we stay silent
and never utter
these limited sounds
called words?

Speak all you want
but draw from that place
where only
silence is heard!

Rest Itself

Unable to understand empty fullness,
mind unaware of what arises there,
instead relies on complex words,
reaching the outer limits of tellurian ken.

~

Waxing poetic eschews the noetic,
a beginning yet a certain end,
seeking the higher using the lower,
with a numinous nod we transcend.

~

Knowledge of the subtlest kind,
beyond contemplation of the mind,
where nothing can invoke or provoke,
shedding you to pass through…

~

Rest here,
rest as…
rest itself.

Not Named

Understanding.

Recognition.

Silence, a symphony.

Space, abundance.

Being knowing
being knowing.

This.

Bliss.

I Shine

Today I stand firm,
as a light
moving through darkness.

I bring hope and comfort
to those who have lost hope
and lack simple comforts.

My flame is brighter in giving away
that which is not mine to possess
yet moves through this vehicle.

The honor to do so is mine,
the outcome belongs to the divine...

I shine!

Incomparable

If you must compare yourself,
spare the body for it is innocent,
reporting what the senses perceive,
working to keep itself in balance,
operating according to its program

~

If you must compare yourself,
spare the mind for it serves you,
taking input from the body
and reporting its analysis,
operating according to its conditioning

~

If you must compare yourself,
hold up your true Self
as you move about this world,
open to be scrutinized by all beings,
a mirror of pure light and love,

...incomparable.

'Up' Rooted

The horizon of the mind
moves in and out,
light and darkness cycling,
revealing and veiling.

Rooted in the body,
a limited viewpoint,
suffering the illusion
of waxing and waning.

This body is investigated,
knowledge to contemplation,
contemplation to knowing,
knowing to Being.

This vehicle, the body,
now known to be
one point of experience,
a gift for a time.

Freed from the flesh,
amidst and among,
ubiquitous Being,
'Up' rooted.

The Funhouse

As children we saw
with fright and delight
creatures revealed
in the dim funhouse light

Mirrors distorted
our reflections within,
some short and squat,
some tall and thin

Others showed faces
contorted and skewed,
with sinister smiles
leering and crude

This playful display
is not all that strange
and should seem familiar
with one minor change

Now the world is the mirror
and the manifest play
configures itself
in our own unique way

Our current experience
of the world we perceive
is shaped by conditioning
and what we believe

Anger sees other,
love sees the One,
when this becomes clear,
the reflections are fun

Actors

Happening happening,
spontaneous appearances
of seamless being

A temporary actor
is created to transact
with an apparent other

Illusory actors borne
of the one seamless being
appear on stage, right on cue

They exchange
smiles and greetings,
interact, play their part

Coins are exchanged
for a cup of coffee,
goodbyes and more smiles

Happening happens,
Illusions melt away,
seamless being.

Resolute

Knowing now what you are,
will you examine this knowing
through the lens of your intellect?

In seeing you are life itself
will you again contract,
feeling separate and divided?

Discovering the truth of space and time
will you cast back and forth,
absent from this eternal moment?

Stop.
Gaze inwardly, still and silent.
Realize again what is here.

I say to you, with earnestness,
do not undervalue this recognition,
remain awake, alert and resolute!

Unknown^th

I sat by a river today
as it flowed toward the ocean
the lifeblood of mother earth,
returning home
for the unknown^th time.

Rain fell lightly, making ripples.
Drops that once seemed separate
joining effortlessly with the river,
merging into oneness
for the unknown^th time.

A dead fish floated by
lifeless and decaying,
flies assisting the process,
scattering it over mother earth
for the unknown^th time.

My reflection peered back
as I studied this unfolding.
This body is marching inexorably onward,
soon to return to mother earth
for the unknown^th time.

The One who observes the return home,
the decay, death and merging
is utterly detached, untouched,
and watches this cycle
for the unknown^th time.

Today

Today allow thoughts
to be seen, springing forth
in the sky of consciousness,
passing like clouds.
Thoughts light and dark,
all change shape and disappear,
leaving the sky without a trace

Today allow words
to arise spontaneously
from the space
of unlimited potential.
Words ringing like bells,
pure melodic vibrations
bypassing minds and
touching hearts

Today allow actions
to originate from a place
prior to mind,
sourced from source.
Actions in service to,
and in honor of others,
collapsing the illusion
of separation

Today offer every
thought, word, action
and outcome
to existence.
Offered in gratitude
for the opportunity
to play in, with and as
the Divine

The Garden of Friends

This garden is growing wild
with friends of varied
color, shape, and size

Each unique in expression,
likened to a flower
sustained by a common sun

While each appears separate,
a deeper connection exists where
unseen roots meet and intertwine

None are 'trying to be'
or forcing growth,
flowering happens

Winter looms,
colors fade,
form collapses

Fear is abolished
in knowing existence delights
to discover and meet itself again

Spring comes,
vibrancy returns,
friendships blossom

Precious Few

Rare are those who truly see
past the outer shell of me

Few can find the hidden place
where shared being has no face

Ones like this don't want a thing
except the company you bring

They help to lift each other higher
by virtue of their inner fire

Their presence can bear silent space
and by doing so, allow for grace

Friends like this are precious few!
I'm grateful for this friend in you.

Grace Embodied

It has been said "What's in a name?"
and this may sometimes be true
but knowing Grace as I do now,
she is Grace through and through

One cannot define what Grace is,
but there are some words from the mind:
open, sincere, shining, bright
boundless, welcoming, attentive, kind

And while the sun may be occasionally veiled,
seemingly gone or out of its place,
it is not and could never be diminished,
its unveiling is due to the existence of Grace

Of course, words are mere pointers
that may come close but not quite,
best find out first-hand when you join us
to experience Grace and bask in her light

A Casual Grin

We've all heard the tales
of scandalous rogues
who sailed the high seas
after adventure and gold

No sovereign held sway
over this motley crew
who followed no laws,
who today now are few

Yet there is one among us
whom I class as thief,
who steals limiting concepts
and exposes beliefs

His disarming way,
with his casual grin
hint at unbridled freedom
of the pirate within

Wisdom that might
come only with age
he expresses so clearly
in word and on page

I admire Charlie's courage
to define his own lot,
he points toward Truth
where X marks the spot!

This treasure he points at
is buried within,
yet I see it shine forth
in that casual grin.

Connected

A hub is where the action is,
a place where friends all gather round,
like-minded individuals form
a community built on common ground

A hub can also represent
a home of sorts for seeking souls,
a place where we can support and lean
and fan these embers into coals

This hub shines light out to the world
acting as a beacon for ones like me,
to guide me safely past the rocks,
safe from samsara, the raging sea

And so, a tribute to my friend Hubbs
my gratitude to him for hearing this call,
the hub who holds this space for us,
whose welcoming presence connects us all

The Show

I am the king,
I reign supreme

I am the slave,
I dare not to dream

I am the prisoner,
I long to be free

I am the jailer,
I hold the key

I am the clergy,
I claim divine right

I am the thief,
I prowl in the night

I am the actor,
I get lost in my part

I am the seeker,
I search for the heart

I am the One,
I direct every role

I sit in the audience,
I watch my own show.

An Open Invitation

Realization of Self,
seeing through false identity,
abiding as presence,
living as this.

~

I encounter those who feel separate,
squeezed into a limited body,
who suffer and project their
inner conflict and pain outward.

~

I remain detached,
an open invitation,
words, deeds, and presence
projecting peace.

~

One who pushes against me
will feel no resistance
and tumble headlong
into themselves.

Passing Through

An open door,
a bright kitchen,
soothing music.

~

Two teacups,
a new toothbrush,
fresh towels.

~

A box of tissues,
a soft blanket,
a comforting nightlight.

~

There are always
clean sheets on the bed
in the guest room of my heart.

The Divine Soliloquy

We gather and sit,
physically distant yet
closer than a bearhug.

The expression of One flows
through a diverse mix of
apparent individuals.

We discuss matters
language cannot describe
yet we understand.

A knowing smile
says more than all the sages
in history have said.

Laughter borne of joy
dissolves separation,
the bearhug tightens.

One troupe of actors,
we take on our roles,
the One playing as many.

The Divine soliloquy,
existence pouring out
into the theater of the world.

Undiminished

On this day,
as with countless days,
many thousands of bodies
began this exploration
and thousands
of bodies fell,
their purpose fulfilled

We honor those bodies
having walked beside them
for a short time,
each a unique vehicle,
a point of view
that lovingly held our gaze
and reflected the same

We called them by a name
and knew their person
for a short time,
a unique expression of
the One being
who experienced and
celebrated existence through them

Their eyes no longer see
and hands no longer touch
yet they have not gone
as they did not arrive,
their changeful aspect ending,
their unchanging reality shining,

...undiminished

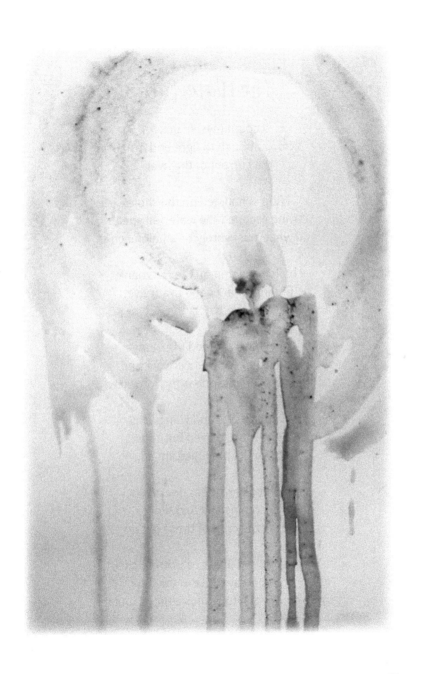

The Waterfall

I count myself lucky,
strong enough to fight and resist
the current of the river.

I flop exhausted on the shore
having escaped the waterfall ahead
and what must surely be a painful end.

I build my camp on the riverbank,
finding what I need to survive,
listless in limbo.

Yet, I have avoided the plunge
and listen as others cry out and
tumble over, disappearing from view.

Time passes and I languish,
the shore barren but safe
from the precipice ahead.

Initially restless, I settle,
becoming still and silent,
hearing the cries of those passing.

Through this stillness I see more clearly,
puzzled by those in the flow
who splash playfully, expressions radiant.

It is then, in the deep silence,
I understand their celebration,
exclamations of excitement and joy!

I feel fear yet know I cannot remain here,
this meager shore-bound existence
is but a resistance to what is inevitable.

I surrender to the flow of the river,
and whoop! with elation as over I go,
falling... into the unknown.

CPSIA information can be obtained
at www.ICGtesting.com
Printed in the USA
LVHW021122090222
710546LV00007B/464